My profile

Name : ______________________________

Phone : ______________________________

E-mail : ______________________________

Month	Income	Expense	Saving	Balance
January				
February				
March				
April				
May				
June				
July				
August				
September				
October				
November				
December				
Total				
			Result :	

Are you satisfied with your financial account?

O Great O Moderate O Bad

90 Days control Expense.

Month______ Year______				
Date	Income	Amount	Expense	Amount
Total				

90 Days control Expense.

Month__________ Year__________

Date	Income	Amount	Expense	Amount
Total				

90 Days control Expense.

Month__________ Year__________

Date	Income	Amount	Expense	Amount
Total				

90 Days control Expense.

Month ______ Year ______				
Date	Income	Amount	Expense	Amount
Total				

90 Days control Expense.

Month ________ Year ________				
Date	Income	Amount	Expense	Amount
Total				

90 Days control Expense.

Month__________ Year__________

Date	Income	Amount	Expense	Amount
Total				

90 Days control Expense.

Month__________ Year__________

Date	Income	Amount	Expense	Amount
Total				

90 Days control Expense.

Month__________ Year__________				
Date	Income	Amount	Expense	Amount
Total				

90 Days control Expense.

Month__________ Year__________				
Date	Income	Amount	Expense	Amount
Total				

90 Days control Expense.

Month__________ Year__________				
Date	Income	Amount	Expense	Amount
Total				

90 Days control Expense.

Month__________ Year__________

Date	Income	Amount	Expense	Amount
Total				

90 Days control Expense.

Month__________ Year__________

Date	Income	Amount	Expense	Amount
Total				

90 Days control Expense.

Month__________ Year__________				
Date	Income	Amount	Expense	Amount
Total				

90 Days control Expense.

Month__________ Year__________

Date	Income	Amount	Expense	Amount
Total				

90 Days control Expense.

Month__________ Year__________				
Date	Income	Amount	Expense	Amount
Total				

90 Days control Expense.

Month__________ Year__________				
Date	Income	Amount	Expense	Amount
Total				

90 Days control Expense.

Month______ Year______				
Date	Income	Amount	Expense	Amount
Total				

90 Days control Expense.

Month______________ Year______________

Date	Income	Amount	Expense	Amount
Total				

90 Days control Expense.

Month________ Year________				
Date	Income	Amount	Expense	Amount
Total				

90 Days control Expense.

Month__________ Year__________

Date	Income	Amount	Expense	Amount
Total				

90 Days control Expense.

Month__________ Year__________				
Date	Income	Amount	Expense	Amount
Total				

90 Days control Expense.

Month__________ Year__________

Date	Income	Amount	Expense	Amount
Total				

90 Days control Expense.

Month__________ Year__________				
Date	Income	Amount	Expense	Amount
Total				

90 Days control Expense.

Month__________ Year__________

Date	Income	Amount	Expense	Amount
Total				

90 Days control Expense.

Month__________ Year__________				
Date	Income	Amount	Expense	Amount
Total				

90 Days control Expense.

Month__________ Year__________				
Date	Income	Amount	Expense	Amount
Total				

90 Days control Expense.

Month__________ Year__________

Date	Income	Amount	Expense	Amount
Total				

90 Days control Expense.

Month__________ Year__________

Date	Income	Amount	Expense	Amount
Total				

90 Days control Expense.

Month__________ Year__________

Date	Income	Amount	Expense	Amount
Total				

90 Days control Expense.

Month__________ Year__________				
Date	Income	Amount	Expense	Amount
Total				

90 Days control Expense.

Month__________ Year__________				
Date	Income	Amount	Expense	Amount
Total				

90 Days control Expense.

Month__________ Year__________

Date	Income	Amount	Expense	Amount
Total				

90 Days control Expense.

Month ____________ Year ____________

Date	Income	Amount	Expense	Amount
Total				

90 Days control Expense.

Month______________ Year______________				
Date	Income	Amount	Expense	Amount
Total				

90 Days control Expense.

Month__________ Year__________

Date	Income	Amount	Expense	Amount
Total				

90 Days control Expense.

Month___________ Year___________

Date	Income	Amount	Expense	Amount
Total				

90 Days control Expense.

Month__________ Year__________				
Date	Income	Amount	Expense	Amount
Total				

90 Days control Expense.

Month__________ Year__________				
Date	Income	Amount	Expense	Amount
Total				

90 Days control Expense.

Month____________ Year____________

Date	Income	Amount	Expense	Amount
Total				

90 Days control Expense.

Month________ Year________				
Date	Income	Amount	Expense	Amount
Total				

90 Days control Expense.

Month__________ Year__________

Date	Income	Amount	Expense	Amount
Total				

90 Days control Expense.

Month__________ Year__________

Date	Income	Amount	Expense	Amount
Total				

90 Days control Expense.

Month________ Year________				
Date	Income	Amount	Expense	Amount
Total				

90 Days control Expense.

Month__________ Year__________

Date	Income	Amount	Expense	Amount
Total				

90 Days control Expense.

Month__________ Year__________				
Date	Income	Amount	Expense	Amount
Total				

90 Days control Expense.

Month__________ Year__________				
Date	Income	Amount	Expense	Amount
Total				

90 Days control Expense.

Month__________ Year__________

Date	Income	Amount	Expense	Amount
Total				

90 Days control Expense.

Month__________ Year__________

Date	Income	Amount	Expense	Amount
Total				

90 Days control Expense.

Month__________ Year__________

Date	Income	Amount	Expense	Amount
Total				

90 Days control Expense.

Month__________ Year__________				
Date	Income	Amount	Expense	Amount
Total				

90 Days control Expense.

Month__________ Year__________

Date	Income	Amount	Expense	Amount
Total				

90 Days control Expense.

Month__________ Year__________

Date	Income	Amount	Expense	Amount
Total				

90 Days control Expense.

Month______ Year______				
Date	Income	Amount	Expense	Amount
Total				

90 Days control Expense.

Month__________ Year__________

Date	Income	Amount	Expense	Amount
Total				

90 Days control Expense.

Month__________ Year__________				
Date	Income	Amount	Expense	Amount
Total				

90 Days control Expense.

Month__________ Year__________				
Date	Income	Amount	Expense	Amount
Total				

90 Days control Expense.

Month__________ Year__________				
Date	Income	Amount	Expense	Amount
Total				

90 Days control Expense.

Month__________ Year__________				
Date	Income	Amount	Expense	Amount
Total				

90 Days control Expense.

Month__________ Year__________				
Date	Income	Amount	Expense	Amount
Total				

90 Days control Expense.

Month__________ Year__________

Date	Income	Amount	Expense	Amount
Total				

90 Days control Expense.

Month ________ Year ________				
Date	Income	Amount	Expense	Amount
Total				

90 Days control Expense.

Month___________ Year___________

Date	Income	Amount	Expense	Amount
Total				

90 Days control Expense.

Month___________ Year___________

Date	Income	Amount	Expense	Amount
Total				

90 Days control Expense.

Month__________ Year__________

Date	Income	Amount	Expense	Amount
Total				

90 Days control Expense.

Month__________ Year__________				
Date	Income	Amount	Expense	Amount
Total				

90 Days control Expense.

Month______ Year______				
Date	Income	Amount	Expense	Amount
Total				

90 Days control Expense.

Month__________ Year__________				
Date	Income	Amount	Expense	Amount
Total				

90 Days control Expense.

Month__________ Year__________				
Date	Income	Amount	Expense	Amount
Total				

90 Days control Expense.

Month__________ Year__________

Date	Income	Amount	Expense	Amount
Total				

90 Days control Expense.

Month __________ Year __________				
Date	Income	Amount	Expense	Amount
Total				

90 Days control Expense.

Month__________ Year__________

Date	Income	Amount	Expense	Amount
Total				

90 Days control Expense.

Month__________ Year__________				
Date	Income	Amount	Expense	Amount
Total				

90 Days control Expense.

Month______ Year______				
Date	Income	Amount	Expense	Amount
Total				

90 Days control Expense.

Month__________ Year__________				
Date	Income	Amount	Expense	Amount
Total				

90 Days control Expense.

Month__________ Year__________				
Date	Income	Amount	Expense	Amount
Total				

90 Days control Expense.

Month__________ Year__________				
Date	Income	Amount	Expense	Amount
Total				

90 Days control Expense.

Month__________ Year__________

Date	Income	Amount	Expense	Amount
Total				

90 Days control Expense.

Month__________ Year__________

Date	Income	Amount	Expense	Amount
Total				

90 Days control Expense.

Month__________ Year__________

Date	Income	Amount	Expense	Amount
Total				

90 Days control Expense.

Month__________ Year__________

Date	Income	Amount	Expense	Amount
Total				

90 Days control Expense.

Month__________ Year__________				
Date	Income	Amount	Expense	Amount
Total				

90 Days control Expense.

Month__________ Year__________

Date	Income	Amount	Expense	Amount
Total				

90 Days control Expense.

Month__________ Year__________

Date	Income	Amount	Expense	Amount
Total				

90 Days control Expense.

Month__________ Year__________

Date	Income	Amount	Expense	Amount
Total				

90 Days control Expense.

Month__________ Year__________

Date	Income	Amount	Expense	Amount
Total				

90 Days control Expense.

Month___________ Year___________				
Date	Income	Amount	Expense	Amount
Total				

90 Days control Expense.

Month__________ Year__________

Date	Income	Amount	Expense	Amount
Total				

90 Days control Expense.

Month__________ Year__________

Date	Income	Amount	Expense	Amount
Total				

90 Days control Expense.

Month________ Year________				
Date	Income	Amount	Expense	Amount
Total				

90 Days control Expense.

Month__________ Year__________				
Date	Income	Amount	Expense	Amount
Total				

90 Days control Expense.

Month__________ Year__________				
Date	Income	Amount	Expense	Amount
Total				

90 Days control Expense.

Month__________ Year__________

Date	Income	Amount	Expense	Amount
Total				

90 Days control Expense.

Month__________ Year__________

Date	Income	Amount	Expense	Amount
Total				

90 Days control Expense.

Month____________ Year____________				
Date	Income	Amount	Expense	Amount
Total				

90 Days control Expense.

Month__________ Year__________

Date	Income	Amount	Expense	Amount
Total				

90 Days control Expense.

Month__________ Year__________				
Date	Income	Amount	Expense	Amount
Total				

90 Days control Expense.

Month__________ Year__________				
Date	Income	Amount	Expense	Amount
Total				

90 Days control Expense.

Month__________ Year__________				
Date	Income	Amount	Expense	Amount
Total				

90 Days control Expense.

Month__________ Year__________

Date	Income	Amount	Expense	Amount
Total				

90 Days control Expense.

Month__________ Year__________				
Date	Income	Amount	Expense	Amount
Total				

90 Days control Expense.

Month__________ Year__________

Date	Income	Amount	Expense	Amount
Total				

90 Days control Expense.

Month__________ Year__________				
Date	Income	Amount	Expense	Amount
Total				

90 Days control Expense.

Month________ Year________				
Date	Income	Amount	Expense	Amount
Total				

90 Days control Expense.

Month__________ Year__________				
Date	Income	Amount	Expense	Amount
Total				

90 Days control Expense.

Month____________ Year____________

Date	Income	Amount	Expense	Amount
Total				

90 Days control Expense.

Month__________ Year__________				
Date	Income	Amount	Expense	Amount
Total				

90 Days control Expense.

Month________ Year________				
Date	Income	Amount	Expense	Amount
Total				

90 Days control Expense.

Month__________ Year__________

Date	Income	Amount	Expense	Amount
Total				

90 Days control Expense.

Month________ Year________				
Date	Income	Amount	Expense	Amount
Total				

90 Days control Expense.

Month__________ Year__________

Date	Income	Amount	Expense	Amount
Total				

90 Days control Expense.

Month__________ Year__________				
Date	Income	Amount	Expense	Amount
Total				

90 Days control Expense.

Month __________ Year __________				
Date	Income	Amount	Expense	Amount
Total				

90 Days control Expense.

Month__________ Year__________

Date	Income	Amount	Expense	Amount
Total				

90 Days control Expense.

Month________ Year________				
Date	Income	Amount	Expense	Amount
Total				

90 Days control Expense.

Month__________ Year__________				
Date	Income	Amount	Expense	Amount
Total				

90 Days control Expense.

Month___________ Year___________

Date	Income	Amount	Expense	Amount
Total				

90 Days control Expense.

Month__________ Year__________

Date	Income	Amount	Expense	Amount
Total				

90 Days control Expense.

Month__________ Year__________

Date	Income	Amount	Expense	Amount
Total				

90 Days control Expense.

Month__________ Year__________

Date	Income	Amount	Expense	Amount
Total				

90 Days control Expense.

Month____________ Year____________

Date	Income	Amount	Expense	Amount
Total				

90 Days control Expense.

Month______ Year______				
Date	Income	Amount	Expense	Amount
Total				

90 Days control Expense.

Month__________ Year__________

Date	Income	Amount	Expense	Amount
Total				

90 Days control Expense.

Month__________ Year__________				
Date	Income	Amount	Expense	Amount
Total				

90 Days control Expense.

Month__________ Year__________

Date	Income	Amount	Expense	Amount
Total				

90 Days control Expense.

Month__________ Year__________				
Date	Income	Amount	Expense	Amount
Total				

90 Days control Expense.

www.ingramcontent.com/pod-product-compliance
Lightning Source LLC
Chambersburg PA
CBHW072210170526
45158CB00002BA/538
9781070383224